PREMATURE

K. Roe

Order this book online at www.trafford.com
or email orders@trafford.com

Most Trafford titles are also available at major online book retailers.

Printed in the United States of America.

ISBN: 978-1-4669-3353-8 (sc)
ISBN: 978-1-4669-3352-1 (e)

Trafford rev. 06/11/2012

 www.trafford.com

North America & international
toll-free: 1 888 232 4444 (USA & Canada)
phone: 250 383 6864 ✦ fax: 812 355 4082

For Kayla, Jenni, Dami and Lauren,
You have lived through this with me.

CONTENTS

For Tio Polo

AUTHOR'S NOTE:

Within this book lie various parts of my soul such as the torn up version, the bitten off version, and the death of many versions. There are not many pieces of my body that I have not self-inflicted on, and this book holds the parts that hold me together. I wear on the outside what is my personal battleground. My scars are past and present imprints that have joined me in my psychological war to find myself and my sanity. These scars are printed on pages now to express the never ending pain and suffering that entails such beings who have felt such things. This book is for anyone who has drowned above land, who has frowned in the sun, or who has stopped beating the normal heartbeat. This book is my soul, cracked and never fully able to heal, yet out in the open for a breath of life.

PREMATURE

In a cough of static
I leave the womb

In a cup of dry guts
I leave the womb

In the beast belly
I leave the womb

Torn from your torso
I leave the womb

Squirming in absence
I leave the womb

Poured in warmed blood
I leave the womb

In my damaged meat
I leave the womb

In a bladder weighed free
I leave the womb

In a blunder of murmurs
I leave the womb

In a prisoner of patience
I leave the womb

In fetal position
I leave the womb

In a breath of the lonely
I leave the womb

In a boneless crib
I leave the womb

With my mouth ill fed
I leave the womb

The birth after
I leave the womb

BUTCHER'S BILE

When I stop to feel
My heart aches
It's a beating bruise
Every pulse is too great

When I stop to feel
My heart breaks
When I've fallen you fall just below
My reflection of self I hold

When I stop to feel
My heart aches
Fallen to the deepest blues
My crystal mouth agape

When I stop to feel
My heart breaks
Sleep doesn't reach me
What brute lies awake

When I stop to feel
My heart aches
Pulse to pulse
My complex flesh

When I stop to feel
My heart breaks
I never loved the purest way
Life in black lost ways

When I stop to feel
My heart aches
My hope falls so very far away
I die when I float awake

When I stop to feel
My heart breaks
I've piled down to broken bones
Yet I cannot leave them to fend alone

When I stop to feel
My heart aches
My pain is growing
And I've never felt weaker

When I stop to heal
I break

THE OPHELIAN ACHE

Do you swallow all this mess
Like I do
Do you see all the rest
Like I do
Do you feel the Ophelian ache
Like I do
Does your mouth pour shadows
Like I do
Do you see your skin burning
Like I do
Can you feel the depths calling
Like I do
Can you bleed from inner mortem
Like I do
Can the sun burn you
As it smiles its warm noose
Do you feel the smiles inviting a hanging
Like I do
Has the weight inside your head
Filled like wet cement
Can you die in her myth
Drown and still feel pure breath
Soft and calm in death
Quixotic in hell's caress
Are you aching like Ophelia
Have you drowned above these grounds
Ophelia and the ache
Had the wretched made you
Am I of the same brood
Because I have drowned for years
I have tried to disappear
I have died too many times
Little deaths that are not seen
They have gone blind
The ache is potent
The ache is grand
Ophelia, we have drowned on dry land.

SYRUPS

I miss them
I need them
And they feel closer
I fall softer
A consequent, you see
So defensive
Can you not blame me
Ashen water
Spare a gentler heart
Codeine marsh
Stained mess, so obscene
I almost feel clean
And I stumble
So full
The batter is raw
Soft crumbs of power
Tastes the mouth
So the coma leaks frosting
A beautiful prophecy to swallow
Not in my bed
Not in my bed

FOOTFALLS

Figments
My carless mind
Swallowed you whole
So you needed someone
Maybe everyone
So many anyones
Melodramatic
Nothing to capture
Failed no other ones
Just the only one
The one I should have loved
Perished soul, my own
To kill a self I've never known
What's left to own
These pills, intoxicants
Anemia, hysteria
The vein, impulses
She climbs an artery
And licks the wine
Poured out a masterpiece

FAMILIAR

Swearing she
Daring she
Such a poison to drink
I've evolved
Should have cremated me
Given the ashes for her to keep
Giving her what I am missing now
See how the abyss sinks aloud
Feel her clutching for nothing
Falling and falling
See her try to bruise me now
Would I let her be bruised too?
That will be the end of me
She will drink me up
And spit me out
One melody at a time.

SICK

I give her no face
She has one heart
I bandage her up
The bandage keeps her apart
The nail is pushing up
Across her beating chest
Tearing up the sown matter
She has left
She had faces
One too many
To rest I gave her none
She needn't a brain
For pain she knew by heart
Now she's scratched out
Herself, a germ.

THE DEAD HOUR

It's in these hours I gossip
To the low
To the dead
Thoughts lie in the air
Verbal ties left unsaid
Waiting, haunting
Pacing around the room
Flooding in my head
These passive glances
Hooks on my bed
Saying what is not said
And crumbling on outside hours
Gossiping in my head
To no one but ghosts
Waiting to figure out
Without a spoken word
Charming to no one
Boredom looms, cradles
Pierces through.

TO PURGE

Don't dance, daddy
You're legs are made of glue
Don't stare, daddy
The crows aren't feeling
Like they use to

Better than throwing down
Better to love our bones
Even better when they're underground

So stay, daddy
I'm listening, aren't you?
Don't play, daddy
That's not as funny as you think it is
I'm not feeling like I use to

And I'm terrified
To bury you
So dig up, I'm still waiting for you.

TWO CENTS, ONE SIDE

Pour out your seriousness
Be honest
We lived a lie
Paint, not a choice
Prefer them, chose you
And they have led me here
Fourth of September
Dare I say November
Rest my head
Shallow illusion of yesterday
Harsh (tip-toe)
And insulted impulse
Gravity is less a qualm now
Fourth of September
Dare I say November
Laying like stones
Fountain of dreams
Can you hear them wish
Can you hear the dreamers pray
Can you believe
Are you still too afraid
What more can they take
Stop hating November.

UNSOUND

As I sit I realize that I cannot cope
It's hard to stutter, let alone say
Speaking to faces
My eyes change in stages
Notion catches nothing
When motions flickers in wait
I divide myself without knowing
Dividing worlds while you're buried
These bones feel quite diseased
While I exist and you are nothing but a memory
Change is my rooted undoing
There in these changes
Is where my heart stops beating
The pain I'm feeling
Shifts heavier until I stop breathing
My chest is severed open
Long lost & sunken down
Away, I can't replace what doesn't remain
Not now, not soon
Not even in the other room
It's not easy to dream with eyes closed
To see you and open my eyes to no sight of you
Still abandoned, still alone
In outside eyes I'm dissolving
For ages now I'm so far away
There is no way to let go
That never was in my control
No way to escape the person you are
The indents, the scars
The sun and the stars
To look in your eyes
And not just see the past.

DOLDRUMS

The stars are closer
I can reach them in sound
The blurry fires in the sky
Pliant to forge tears out my eyes

The illusions have clouds
They color my eyes
They deny me

I walk in the sand
Part waiting, receiving
Impeccable, you in your liar bed
You are not veritable

These illusions long
They can't be right
When you deprive me

Will you just look up
See the partial hangman
Out of my insides
Leaking ghosts

The illusions I made on my own
They pacify me
I should face them.

SEASONAL

Plush, licking my mindless drain
Albeit caress a little minty mess
You really crashed down
And left me tumbling down the abyss
Ripped and damaged
A priceless homage
Swallowed 15 white little pills
Magnet filled with similes
And felt nothing for too damn long
I walked until I basically fell empty
It's not you I'm missing
Hollow and beating, wetter with blood
They sprinkle like lactating eyes
As destructive if not worst
On wavering methods to stay afloat
Half mind and body too tired
To think things through
So impervious to our ailments
So you sit and judge, as all saints do
And as grief watches and tumbles down
Spring, our deadly rose bud season
The summer ache
Half way fallen on falls bedroom window
Those ropes in the winter grieving.

ANESTHETIC

Pictures die like the wind
Orphaned
Something's, they change
When you went down
My hands held your cloud
He never told me how bad it stung
The flesh eating mouths
Sorest held at the tip of his breath
Collapsing onto him like a mausoleum
Taking that heart of his
Into the drum of death
The withering that can escape no man
Not even him
Something's, they change
When you went down
I'm left clutching your grave

NO PULSE

The skies low on air
You don't breathe
And when I feel you
I miss you
And when you die
I'm with you
Dropped gloves,
I see you
Heart thump
I wish you
Would go up and stay.

There's a night where
I'm reminded
There are floods
I wash away with you
I drop my hand
I didn't use to
My blood's cold
I didn't need to
I'm lying awake
I wish you
Would go up and stay.

I hear a sound
I wake you
I think I'd die
Without you
I'm just held over the moon
To drag away from you
I fell asleep
Knowing it's not true
And I blink
I wish you
Would go up and stay.

BURIAL

Hello
You who can't see
Who has no depth
Have you awakened?

Hello
You who can't breathe
With eyes so deep
The skin cracks at the skull

Hello
You who can't motion
The echoes are faint
The echoes blind

Hello
You who can't stay
Your handprint saw day
I took your crackled palm

Hello
You who can't remember
Brian matter is no matter
So who am I talking to?

Hello
You who have no say
How do you reply?
Your voice thick as gravel

Hello
You who are away
I visit you in trauma
You pull me down.

ELDEST YOUTH

Death buries her claws on my footsteps
Hoping to claw down my partial flesh
My skin boils down to ill matter

Torn down and battered like a soul
Slipping away, down to hell we go
Cradling my heart as we pass every edge

The glass eye watches like a judge
The heartbeat spun towards no sun
To dream in dreamless speed

To a pattern of dead plastic wings
The innocence of feathered swans
In a pool of my only wilted root

Buried under the dirt, mounds of it
Somehow it's easier to drown in it
To offer my weight underneath its core

Bless the air with my stench no more
I've come and gone and come undone
Bleed with me and let it be done

I've lived for years in my skin
Ran for days in my youth, carried by the wind
And now carried on my death bed

It's been building up this sweet sound
The flesh for pound in perfect symphony
I've earned my way out.

THE DWARF HOME

Take me back
Towards orphaning
Filling fluids
Aborting

Bring me back
Towards my toddler feet
Pink Stubs
Forming

Leave me
Stop the packing
Feet unmoved
Unraveling

Dig me up
Stop your whining
Placing flowers
Becoming

Drag me out
Crawling through stages
White lines
Reforming

Keep me alive
She's wandering death
Go to sleep
Save her

Light my cigarette
Some months clean
It never stops
Recovery.

CHOKED ASPIRIN

Swollen sprinkles, fallen skies
Candy so rotten, drenched in lies
We speak on empty pockets
When your thirst starts to die
Swallowed by sugar mountains
Follow to our demise
Pray for sunrise, I can't save you
So many sweet hallucinations
Sold, they sedate you
No-one needs to bother
Walk down the full-dazed pond
I let his ghost come home
I was so uninspired
I was ready to devour my opiates
To leave my own consciousness
It feels a lot slower
And for how much longer
Do I have to stay sober.

VALIANT

Such a dumb infection
My guts so red and tempered
Halves, to my own rationalization
Counsel the imperfect
When your perfect expressions
Taste rejected
Cold like a bruise
Swollen, swallowed and chewed
Feet stand unclever
Heart itself
My hands, scratching
Won't let nobody take me home
Lies ablaze
Push another hair from my face
Like you're not clawing it out of me
Almost hard to do nothing
The pain hurts much more
As I try to relax
My lower back feels wise
Slight cracks up my sides
Rip it heavenly
Rip it raw
Stick the vitamin
Like it will help at all.

ECLIPSED

So many raptured moons
Tears in my eyes
We break our other halves down
Let the dam sweep over
Pull us over
As when the sun comes up
She'll wipe us dry
But raptured moons
Don't hang so high
Dark months gravitated
Seethe beneath our heavy hearts
We searched for land everywhere
But no one checks the sea
Our mouthful fills down under
A gutless symphony, glitter membrane
Shatter those velvet pieces
I have sown around my wrists
Repair, repair
Eyelashes aware
So deaf to your stare
It's not like I'm breathing anymore
Not for you, not for you
Strapped to the pupil
Raging like a crow
Above my bed
Thorazine inbred
Just like it has before
Those pills don't change the places
Dragging me sorry
Can't bleed the blood I was to adore
Sated, so, so sore.

ERODA

Drag my wings down like an abyss
A moth in depth of colossal damage
I wait endless years to bleed anew
The sadness stains
We ate those wings to bury us
Death spots me in her rotten eyes
Pains heated tar, blackened dye
Makes a gash as if I
No more rotten than ever before
My oldest friend: agony
Coldest friend
Cotton, cotton, cotton
The welt I leak from is plentiful
Until these eyes swell
A white light burnt holy grail
A candle, no
The grass gets greener
And they say I am much cleaner
Flayed, perfectly obscene
Just to all that won't see

PHANTASMAL

Do you see the hook?
Can you tell I'm starving?
For something explicit
A naked force, I die
Smoked acid, purify
A better lie

And you see
And you cave
Plain sand man
Leaving mess on my rug
Come down a while
I'm not going to last here alone

I caught you for free
A lampshade too bright
Are you blurred out now?
You never freed of me
The sad stains are the best I bleed
Inhuman wake

Can you sedate these mirrors
Looking back at me
It's hard to push myself away
When they watch
And all they see
The emptiness I've held like greed

CLOTHED

Puncture
The blood of the heart
My tomb of ruin
I'm half grown

Puncture
The blade of the heart
So we hide ourselves
Look at you

Puncture
The age of the heart
Pure like spewed coma
Does it come off me in waves

Puncture
The rage of the heart
Spinning like an automatic
Was I the nature of regret

Puncture
The death of the heart
Too many bodies
Crash down on me

Puncture
The land of the heart
Ruby bleak
I soaked for hours

Puncture
The meat of the heart
Keep yourself clothed
Will I ever stop screaming blood.

CONSTANT

I breed a word
Swollen around the edges
Barley even mended
The bruise has gone soft pink to royal blue
Pollen redecorates the puncture
Kept, I've dried up
All is fallen asteroids at my feet
Empty dull memories on cigarette buds
Trailing from my soul to the sun
Embody my dismemberment
The fountain faucet drips like watered nights
Where my bed drowns my eyes
Modern medicine flowing like cocaine
Through my veins in the dark
Heartbeats pained for decades
And I am awake for days
In the bloodied wake of incented rain
The rain of plush sweat dried pain
The pulse of dead men walking dazed
Cerebellum, quiet speeding drain
Calm your pulsing stampede
The beat of hooves rushing down my brain
The darkest days have pinched every scab
As stone as I can go
The wound is not marble
I shrivel to hushed down breath
The coldest ashes I've lain upon
Soft enough they claw
Frail enough to soak me up.

BRILLIANT

If the blood explodes
Let it leak
My eyes once dawned
Now soured empty
The past licks idly
Beside my brow, imprisoned
And the sky reigns
Off the top of my lungs
The cough of dead men
And the hearts of the young
The blue butcher bury
The calm and nervous year
The trees tripping over
Said words they never tell
Asleep and cradled
In arms I never felt
My lips bloom raspberry
Crackled angels in parted lines
As my body shivers of impact
My scalp is plowed
Memories laying their prints
Escaping in my mind
Dampening my tired ebb
An echo dropped on tile
Waves dripping
Like a bothered sink.

PRUNE

Soft yellow, plum maroon
A thousand screams
My body etched, in bloom
Feathered light fingerprints
The darkest prints
On humble flesh
Soft, the blood root
Tainted little sculpture
My body sticks like glue
What body of mine, broken
What body of yours, bruised
My body lays a torch
In flames, a dress
In torn abuse
What ligaments indeed
Were my own to soothe
I bathe to gain a breath
To wash away the crude
Fill the prints with oil
To paint a pretty wound
One I can call my own
One I can forget if I choose
And cut this fresh meat off
Before my lips are ink
Spitting out the ooze
That I painted away
Pouring my aches
Out into this room
My blood once pale
Before my shape
Now blood bruised.

SOAKED OAKS

Bruised and unfolding
From tree and bark
I suffer my age
A belly quivering of ache
My bones, limbs of pure dispose
The outsides stain through my skin
My pre-state
Fills of moss
And linger only when the earth quakes
Her teeth un-fruitful
Eyes soft like rain
I place my bags on the ground
Here in her maze
So I count the circular mounds
Under the heiress eye
The bodies are painted
All along her thighs
The maze lithe
Her bruises are all inside.

SOUL CONTAINER

Container
He shamed her
Never recovered
Never returned the favor
Lost container

Soft spoken
Heart broken
Neither part heart of a person
Not a villain, but not much a sinner
She was a lost container

Everything is self-absorbed
Fake fateful image of my trembles
Secret walk in rocks, toe blunder
Stateless emotion, I should have woken
That pretty lost container

I lost my container
She was never about the season
Another world is hers, so shameless
I lost my own container
So selfless.

A PARTING

There's a rocky road in front of me
These shoes fit someone taller than me
I'm nestled in fear
I tremble every step
The dark road etches in my footsteps
Unreliable to most—
I was here.
I pull my coat closer
Wrestle the demons clawing here and there
I'm almost halfway nowhere
If I close my eyes
Would I waver onto unwanted land
Should I fear you more than deaths own hand?
I walk in faint indents
On this belly founded gravel
Don't know where I'm to go
Some footsteps I've stood ghost
Unreliable to most-
I was here.

STAIRS

I look
There is nothing there
To satisfy—a joke
Would you mind?

Soft steps
They rise to my own
Crippled like a tree
Where to move?

Did they desperately try?
I won't see
I trade those, you know?
Still they don't change

All thes stairs
Can I reach the one I see?
The one they made
For everyone but me.

PREHEAT

If you don't go away I will eat you
Shatter your silk flesh nail to limb
Your shadow face, half lived
I am so tired my bones sing
Ageless hours tick by, watering mouths
I'm wasted like batter on the kitchen top
Boiling majesty, crevice rave
Soft trailing like a runaway train
Your white teeth look too good
I find myself a bad companion
Overlooked, I'm better off friendless
My sweet debris
It cradles ill thoughts from wandering
As it springs through
My insides thrive to speak
Torn from my illusionary sweat
In forms clawed down my sides
Parted sea, the dams broken wide
Salt liquor bathing.

DRY LEAFS

My soul is tired, it wants retreat
My skin decays, goodbye broken meat
I feast on weather far from kind
I play the tape faster, forward, rewind
The impending has belittled me
My undoing will be of soft noise
Bringing the calm in violent song
My mind has spun in circles
Front to back in constant rhyme
Whatever devils have emerged
Wordless bounds to tie me to dark binds
And I bleed all the way down
Until my feet swirl crimson and weight
To where no land is quiet
And no me is a pleasant me
The blackened root approaches
Tastes at my flesh, licks like a raw apple
Swarming darkness with his glass eye
Mirroring my madness
I pile it on of mass and lazy imprints
Gradually descending
Inhaling at illness like a sponge.

CABBAGE

Time in-between
They catch up to me
And the dawn is late
Gravitated
Cold and boldly dazed my mind
The fire genocide
Another solvent now
Extravagant, even (for me)
The burned tongue
Just like blood
Bruised and swollen
The beating crush
So I could tend to the photo
So many watered almosts
To torch those faces and never know
Like my own shelved insomnia.

BRAIN MATTER

I look out, the haze scares me.
The level has borrowed the lesser me
So I face the baggage, packed up
So we leak of presence
Naked being, non-existing conflicts
Pierce me out of my sight, the sifting
Not meant for me, scrambled like infection
Everything I reach, I clutter
Go forward, mark a corner
Stoned far from comfort
Even the new insides still hollow
Not real, no feeling or light
So home's a something more stolen than ripe
My plague is set
My strongest leak in years
I welcome his dark void
Open eyes & yet I drown
I still can't reach you, I can't comply with wonderment
I never found a sound below
I see all your selfless mess, I did it to you
These days are fake, these days burn a fake burn
Home, like a casket
So I over-reacted.

SPLIT MORNING

Split in oceans
Tired of wailing
Momma said it's not even raining
Get out, get out

Plain as the day
Coming out, waiting
Of these delusions I am engraving
Get out, get out

Withering around
Got those wounds in my mouth
My lips start fading
Get out, get out

Reborn to nothing
My head's so thick
Swarming down to the rain
Get out, get out

Hollow out my breath
I've seen these ashes
I've been born in your crypt
Get out, get out

I feel your eyes
Dampened and alive
Bringing out the divine
Get out, get out

I feel the shadows
They are inhaling
Down my neck I feel them saying
Get out, get out.

POST

Stand to this rhythm
That has no face
I cover these blinds
Where this haze originates
The sound, the light
I am something I create
Is that what you can't see?
Befallen, the bleakest wound
I've ever seen
Keep yourself clothed
Blood red, brutal rose
I know, I know
But that bullet hurt like hell
I see those eyes
I see that look
I see no soul
The hook is useless
To fill spaces I no longer know
Pictures flayed in the fire
I wilt in the non-summer bloom
You think 'She's made of them'
It's all easy when we forget.

AFTERGLOW

Trauma, the beat
Liquor, the limbs
Fire, the words
Death, my roots

Castles are singing
They've brought love home
What is this feeling
Wait, I can't watch

Trauma, a hand
Liquor, my wrist
Fire, self-spun
Death, silent

It takes a love
To finally sink up
The rim of placid snow
Wait, I feel

Trauma, neck
Liquor, bruise
Fire, sour glory
Death, hold me

The sign of you
The star of truth
Never said I waited
Wait, I'm lonely

Trauma, selfish
Liquor, blood
Fire, a son
Death, obliterated

For the thought of was
Where I ought to be
I can see your face in mine
Wait, no apologies

Trauma, confusion
Liquor, abused one
Fire, eating the blame
Death, we are one

Way up high
Rain in damp skies
Draining self-decay
Wait, don't wash his rain off me.

EYELESS

It's horrible
I can't look at you
Any(one?)
Go, far away
Gone now?
No whispers
No aches
Soft ashes scale for miles
These bones have no relief
Was it odd?
How we did go
So far away now,
Go
And just once
With dying eyes
I felt your motion squeak
These thoughts stop emerging
What do I do (did I do)
Gone, gone
So far away, now
My air, soul deserted
Miserable
Buried deep
So constant
Never whole
Liquid I cease to forgive
A fools glory.

BEAST AND HEART

Weakened hearts braved
Cradled marsh of ether
Sweet gallows platoon
Hours of cool death
Crouched, and hours claim
Body temperature so unclean
Blood flows, unearthing
With my frail thorn crown
Ever red, my wine for bread
I look at you, porcelain and all
My tongue goes thick
There are gallons of razors
Hidden under your bed
I'm waking up about to devour
The harm is swarming
Melodramatic instances
Close my eyelids tight
Blind sedative
Blood of the beast
And heart of the corpse
Swarming in pulse
Bred in a bottle of nerves
Ripping my flesh
Sticking wings to my skin
My burn is unique, you blazed
Sore ache, a triumph
The lungs are cold
My breath stains the window
Warm mass, sad shadows
I take calm mouthfuls
I sails the sail of sober wounds

PLAINS BELOW

White bellied granite
Bellies of stone
The crater in your heart
Revels my own
In the bleakest crown of winter
Wherein dusk will surely grow
Where not an angel can brush my shoulder
From my perishing frozen fingertips
To my foul hearted nerves
I see what only I hold
The plains below
And I gasp at the deepened roots
How every buried shiver shows host
And ground my feet down to their hole
I've been washing the years off
Freshly picked off my marrow
Those delinquent icicles
What if my best is not enough
What if it wreaks the land I swallow back
My mouth shut holds a world of sorrow
The same sorrow I grew on my own
A pain growing through the moments
The abundant growth of painted bones
Painted cleverly to rot every winter
Colder than the cruelest cold
I shiver a grief, my death
What gift every part of my heart has let go.

CREATURES

Creatures, bowel of souls
Creatures, rolling up their sleeves
Creatures, sleeping at my knees
Creatures, standing way too close
Creatures, acting as my ghost
Creatures, overreacting
Creatures, protective and dazzling
Creatures, far from well
Creatures, a story to tell
Creatures, knocking in my head
Creatures, starving in my bed
Creatures, catching my teardrops
Creatures, waiting out in the fog
Creatures, blood speaking tongues
Creatures, resting in my lungs
Creatures, scarring my foul arms
Creatures, taking violent root
Creatures, the distance to pain is truth
Creatures, the truth lies for you
Creatures, my lonesome knights
Creatures, without abandon
Creatures, developing like fruit
Creatures, we leave no ruin
Creatures, with bitter aftertaste
Creatures, with pills to sleep
Creatures, dead at my feet
Creatures, my annihilation
Creatures, a figment of my imagination.

DOE EYED

Far from home
Apart of God, towards no sky
Belief is no friend of mine
Doe eyed, stilled

In partial mate
I marry his creaking core
Punctured like a sore vein
Doe eyed, stilled

Equivalent bastards, cowards
You hold no gag to my teeth
Bitten like a breakfast meal
Doe eyed, stilled

Jealous feathered mane
I owe no turbulent feet a brain
No pain
Doe eyed, stilled

Barren, taken
Pull my abdomen from my skin
Wretched crown
Doe eyed, stilled

Fresh and faint
Buried in these forgotten trees
I search for and through
Doe eyed, stilled

Mother Marsh
Supply none plenty
Water, water
Doe eyed, stilled

Wander, I wander in thee
Doe eyed and scared to breathe
Doe eyed, parted ventricle
Doe eyed, stilled.

DILATED PUPILS

Dilated Pupils
I cannot see
Burn these eyelashes
Witch, you have my face

I can barely breathe
Make these eyes look sane
Make them cold, so they know I'm not awake
And I can feel you
White dusted room, inhale

Dilated pupils
Draw me crooked
Poke me with your hooks
Witch, you have my face

I can't breathe
I feel closer to mortal
When I seize
And I can't feel you
White dusted room, awareness

Dilated pupils
I slither into my dress
My blood depressed
Witch, you have my face

I don't breathe
Paranoia in the breeze
I know this scene I am borrowing
Dragging me down to the hole in my bed
White dusted room, emotion

Dilated pupils
You see the lines in my face
To be where I am there is no me
Witch, you have my face

I won't breathe
I won't feed into these realities
My black faint hail is entrancing
White dusted room, carelessness.

THE TRAIN RIDE

Sewer brain
The eyes stray
Onto the clash
Bodies

Perishable
Quote the asteroid
Sitting beside me
We burn

Mold
Breathe in
Stuffing
Whole dried dirt

Worn
Like a black belly
In the dolphin coffin
Wanted

Tear the bread off
The skin
Comes off
Soft like butter

Cruel
Dead internal organ
Is the taste
On my tongue

Tangible
Rope sticks
Around the neck
Cradle of duress

My sweat flakes
I'm blood curling
Overtaking
Leaving the nest

I weep
In the parallel high
Creature lie beside
Me when I've ruin.

SULFURIC

Teardrop, pink pearled eye
Searching through powderless skies
Softly married
Defaced like my own parade
Ashamed, no worth
So cheek, and wild
Pouring every sunrise
Soreness, my only family
Tear them wide open
From here, now and then
I open you
So now I lick my own abuse
So many
So they know
My own dead resident
Encaging my real eye
So knifed
Enemy of my own saliva
My printed milk
No redness.

IN THE AIR

You leave me stranded
Held by a crooked bandage
Oh, the irony
Gone away
Back to my cage
Pulsed, I aged for days
I face my own asylum
You who pull at my veins
The little stem cells
Would this taste ever fade
Saved in my head
These feelings feel full drugged
Time flies and never waves
They count the pages
Read the constant stages
They take my eyes
Until my eyes go blind
Thanks to you
I find these eyes aren't my own.

DEAREST MORNING AFTER

The haze has yet to disassemble itself
The soft pitter patter of drained water
Falls like thunder on my clouded ears, it crawls
Dormant until it finds a reason to haunt me
Cold bones have shaken the life from my flesh
Its tantalizing breath sticks to my neck
It causes the air to dampen with delight at my undoing
I cradle in my form, now in pieces
Drained to the sickest stem
An ought right chuckle of bitter song and breathless mouths
I bind myself together with ribbons of self-doubt and awareness
I am weary of where my mind has roamed
What fields does it reside in
What pastures has it died in
If there was a death worth following
Would I trip on my way down?
I drop below my unwell fever
To the unnamed which the seams untie themselves
My sleeves unwoven and unguarded
I will offer up sore wounds
I am without cause at this time of uncertainty
What other pound of flesh can I pour out for you?
Stems of my nervousness ache to their pressure points
To relive all the clots in time, these deaths of mine
Carnivorous these words are
Licking at my barely healed flesh
My black belly swells at these parts
Parts I have left behind
To you I assume I had no right
My veins curl up in this skin I am wearing
What flesh eating monster have I let loose?

PARTS

The scar on my hands
It's got teeth marks
Sober vermin
In my insomniac sack
What exactly was my excuse
I rushed to self-abuse
Down my own inner tube
So I divorced my own value
I never loathed the murderer
Like you thought of me
I can't control what's coming over me
No more excuses
My attempts
My bare knuckled scars
My flesh inside
Rip my belly and put me under
Bruise the sickness inside of me
You think is because of you
I was the one who lost
I was the one who lost
I was the one that needed to be removed.

CHARRED

Watered
Watered down
Like a grave
Old and gray
Like a baby
Fingers feel so artificial
Shaded
Shaded glass
Spun in my head
My spider web
Like a defect egg
I drowned
Watered down
Gagged, and just never found
Monday Morning
Souless, like a dirty mattress
Don't use water
Smothered
Grief, savor the taste of my torment.

COLLISION

You are the smoke in my lungs
The fresh flesh in my wound
The blood in my blue veins
The gravel on my tomb
You burn my throat with gasoline
You are the tar above my eyelid
You are the pain in my heart
The devil in my soul
You are the breath of agony
You are the giver of lost omens
You are the dance of the beheaded
The blade pressing down on ill wrists
The bread of mold under my sink
The lack of health I breathe
You are the seed of my disease
You are the land of my memories
You are the birth of my demons
You are made up of healed scars
The bandaged crackled ones speak
You are the meal I purge
You are the swollen hunger I need
You are the careless binger of pain
The wilting scent of my sanity
You are the cruel sided army
You are sucking the person out of me
You are the truth burnt in irony
The dark pit in my stomach as it churns
You are the drunk that pieces me together
You are the collision, I am the road

SAVORING

Can I pull it out
Or will it reach back in
I'm flickering burnt ashes
The air I inhale screeches
Take a bitter pill
Until the feeling ceases to swell
Until the butcher punches the clock
Beating silenced hell
Will my head stop thundering
To my crooked sight
In this darkness I have no feet
I crawl through a clouded daze
Feeling the nothing of yesterdays
Sweeping into now
And I plead over gently
Without making a sound
In a much too calmed mantra
I bleed it out in pounds
I can never speak in tongue
My belly is too full
And if I try to breathe it out
My heart threatens revolt
If I had more courage
Or if I had more ounces of myself
Perhaps this dealing would run by mouth
And my hands would stop aching
My jaw would stop clenching
My blood would stop answering
To my every wavering hour.

SANDMAN

Dreams, for seconds lying waste
In a language of discarded thoughts
Alive and awake behind an eyelid
Rebirth in the wake of a closed eyelid
Seldom my escape in the crook of imagery
The hands that grasp and hold on
The echoes that breathe inside
Leak on these internal walls
And a savage swamp these lakes are
Such sure downward spirals
That they have made me fall
Dreams, for little dreams
I've had them all
A dream is harder to hold
When dreams start to feed you off
We dream of dreams
We hold them to our heart
What a dream I dream
Dreams where I fall
To where I am left
With no heart at all
The pleasantry of my dreams
Is I wake with only the dream
Only the dream sleeping within me
Sometimes I'd wish I'd never dreamt at all
My dreams have slept in me
Some would say I've slept far too long.

HOME

Quiet sting on
The burden tree
Try to keep the dressing
Falling from me
My heart breathes empty
Burning breeze
Two A.M. I'm stirring
Feel the creeping
I'm in my lake of salt
Itching from the dream
That climbs through me
Eye slithering the soul off me
A swelling like a thorn
My mouth jolts open
I try to keep the worlds
From sailing free
They'd cry a storm
That would only bleed
If they truly know
The broken piece in me
I look down the drain
It's watching me
I brought my loving arms
And they cherry bleed
So I wash my sweet ounce
And carry my gauze to sleep
Hide it down so they
Won't hardly ever grieve.

REDDING

The lunging
Terror waited for you
Lingering threats on her beak
Tempering to the weak
And laying her body down

Films and years
Cradled to your side
Fumbling through passages
Half eaten and barely alive
Dragging corpse—obliterate me

The butterfly skin
Mimics in earsplitting voice
A havoc of imagery
Knocking me down
And flying away

We eat at the marble table
Sitting as if we were cradled
And every feast as bitter as gravel
For me, the food is toxic
I crave the feast of the empty

To retire is a wound
Time handles the deepest scars
Time waggles its tongue
Licks a poison of heart
To my mumbling lips

The cancer in my eye
Holds the burning bits dry
Of what I can no longer stomach
Of what I can't let die
The boulder of my insides.

SCARLET

I amputate myself
My ears drown out
With self-hatred in my heart
Breathing inhaled
Versions of myself
Through the years
I am not satisfied
Other than faceless
Carrying on
My bitter word breath
My notes play no sound
I am worse than a dead rat
To chew on
I try to color on my nose
To see if I fit here
In a new day, in a new year
I have better hope in no days
I am a better self with no name
I am a fond disappearance
Yet I am not wishing
To go far from here
Where I am
There is no more pretending
It's become a blood sport
Protecting me from little old me
Resisting rescue
Flying with no dreams
Some things crash
Burn into the deep
Left out the magnets
Wretched them from me
Reign me loose.

EDEN

I feel black of heart
What if it doesn't happen?

The bleeding truth of art
When the sun lives in spite of me

The little rumble
Blades sliding down the cheek

Fingers tightly typing
As big as my thumb

My very plastic one
Kind of collapsed

I was spun like a memory
Revealing and dusting off the rotting sun

Away I sway
You and the summer haze

The gun clock
Enlightening, is it not?

Ticking for revival
Recall that the body does in fact fall

How the hole in my head
Doesn't solve anything at all.

SANITARY CONFINEMENT

Syringe, of lovely pointed affection
Due to your royalty
Feasted on a platter as simple as you
Fleeting all thought and ravaged platoons
The sleeper placates jumping within the glass room
Temptation, full attention in the dreamless illusions
Acting in complete oblivion
A manic child in vein, of blood
These trips toward black sponge swamps
I tremble in sickly waters, petrified waters
They who have never felt me trudge into their arms
Taken a fool in plastic body parts
I leak a scent of the dead
Welcome to me, you unwelcomed friend
Pressed into my coils in ravenous greed
For what I once was ill tempered
Your vice has sickened my open ends
And I can't weather your open voyage
Today as it seems I stand far too deep in your grasp
The nearest sight, I am alive to burn
Those raining nights have lived on longer than me.

SOBER

And if you burn me
Burn my soul
What's left of it (bodies)
No beat, no pulse
You have dragged it out of me
My skin, yours to dissect
Another stolen theft
Another dosage
The edible restraints
Never sober, never over.
Cold like a gutless savior
Your breath, so human
Not like a savior
Not like a savior.
Like a killer
My sin to a sinner
The less you swallow
The less to abort, come tomorrow.

SATED SORES

When the pain starts to ooze its way
Bruising your heart at the root
The self-inflicted name
Drink it away
And it burns down your jugular waste
As if it was yours anyway
Soft rotten weight
Cursed the light and the day
So I create lulled decay
Weak inebriated haze
The self-inflicted game
Drink it away
The binge of regret in every taste
My blood runs bold
So thick and punctured
My heartbeat lands its breath
Along an iron tongue
Licks the roof of my mouth
The weight of loss is dull
The self-inflicted stain
Drink it away
And it swirls, sweet devil juice
Throat and brain
A careful solace without pain
The self-destruct button
Push, plush escape
Until the eye sways a little
And the legs give away
Until the sickness is spewed on tile
Until the bowel has no say
The self-inflicted vein
Drink it away
Partly stranded with no self
Fresh gauze in place
Daylight slices at the skin
Like a ill infected blade
The brain is a coma
The dread presses its face
Of pressured daylight agony
I self-inflicted
I drank my pain away.

AID

Our cheap fed mouths
Scented breath of our genetics
We sway to anti-psychosis
And we end up broken

Walk down your isle
Sweet yellow prescribed mellow ethers
We crawl under veins like heroin
I took that anti-psychotic too

I fell down that abyss like you
Nothing left but scar tissue
Soft marble mania
Plastic puncture pistol

Spit up earth bile
Cause you see the taste before your eyes
I crawled under those veins
I took the same anti-psychotic as you.

SELF-TAUGHT

I am left to my own devices
I am left to wander the depths of the world I see
I'm not crazed as I have been
I've just held it close
The craze is beneath these bones
I can carve you out a piece
Be dead and ugly as me
Feel pain as if there was no other being
Or remember nothing but what I've seen
What I've spoken is not what haunts me
What is walking freely in my sight
The walking enemy
I can't release that enemy
I've taught her everything.

ROBIN

There
Tantalizing flesh
What do you pour out
A pouring mess
A field of gloom
Tulips on the moon
On your rotting mouth
Buried in your cocoon
For forests of death
I came along
Ripped out your sutures
Rid red to the bone
Strong strokes of armor
Became mine to dampen
To be born empty
To live it out
In color, beheaded company
With your sour taste
All your dry wilted sighs
Echoing above the mountains
Entwining in my hair
Pushing forward like a drug
Inner calming but unwell.

HALVES

I should have known
Not to wake up today
The dreams, now they follow me
Bring me to a place far from reality
Inside enveloping teeth far from mourning
I see the grief stare into my skin
The eyes rip a resting place into my orbs
Losing my mind to a land of no space
No joy, no me, no other living thing
And when heart starts to obliterate
What a flayed being this heart speaks
We have joined for lasting misery
We're crippled with everyone, everything
Two minds, one soul
Breaking like a hatching egg
Skin turned foul, rotting away
The stronger it churns every day
I can't keep the wandering pupil
With the hostess that never sleeps
These foreign parts have made a home of me
Nothing changes except the scenery
The blinding pain sees right through me.

PALLID LAPSE

So I swam among the raptures
I stained indecent sobrieties
To my own
I should have mopped up
As the destroyer
My cravings never fill
No shell to crawl or claw out of
Glossy cave of defects
Kissing the fractures
I licked the bandage clean
I've washed the drought to death
Like a silent apocalypse
Out in the precious sea eyed cream
All our sails
Undressing.

CARNIVAL CARNAGE

Stolen pounds of pearls
Eyes a black swirl
Half Invitation
To watch me crawl
The mother's milk
Never helped at all
Poisoned throat burns
No, the mother's milk
Never helped at all
Poseidon's silk
Tastes cheap
Virus guillotine
Poured out, defiled
Like newborn blood
Sowing black fetal crowns
Saw him lie her down
Swirls in the devils' curls.

SHARPS

Torment
Your cat slit eye
Your webbed feet
Crystalized dye

Sometimes I run
Straight through the pills
And no one knows
No one knows

Hide the knife
My ovary seed
They remove my . . . (placenta drip)
And the sickness is carried away

Don't talk
There's no one there
Do I have to strap you down dear?
They slay no safe injury

Conform, Conform
Don't lie down and sink
Down the drains where no one stays
As if I have any other place

It hurts only when I move
When the bolt shocks me alive
No one knows
No one knows.

ACID RAIN

Guilt soft
Under the sedative
Melting against floral sheets
Pale core seclusion
Cutting out empty shells
Sticky fairy cream
Sell the person next to me
Lost in some degree
Almost safe in limbo
Aborted to the skin I own
Bandage all over my deep ends
All the world can do
To patronize me
My nemesis meat
Fluttered bed pans
What aborted tissue
Will they clean
On those shelves

FILTER MONA

The clutter is escaping
Like the boneless
Thickness of your eyes
The rational mind
Deceit of inner speaking
Distinct in the illusions you set free
Abused, like your soul
We purge
You should have waited
I would have been the enemy
Pave these scars
With anxious feet
There crawl our alibies.

ADORE A PHOBIA

You abandon my relief
Set a glow aflame
And when I'm away
You are outpouring all of our pain
You set these stories
Higher than manmade atrocities
But it's already plain disbelief to me
That when you're afraid to fly
You're not going to climb that many steps
To get away from falling
The window is already far too high
All of your memories
They're all out on those windshimes
They left you far behind
So you're not going to jump
When you can fly
And you don't need to climb
When you've been left behind.

MOONSHINS

Sad mantel
Four diseases
Can't beat me so special
Found a heart with wire
Means so much more to them than me

We make so many days
Catch up on these hollow graves
My speechlessness
Astonishment and recycled birth

Follow my expression
I have the last prescription
We left to the faithful
Knew he'd leave us all
It was so sad

We made so many sand castles
Catch up to me when you float away
My adoring lies
Astonished and still a has been

Should these hands create myself
So far from self-restraint
We make my eyes
For the first time I feel pain

Shame on me
Stain on me
Shame on me
Stain on me
On my hate soup.

CORALLINE

For all my lies
For all my convictions
For all my conquests
My heart slayed before your eyes

I did not dry this moment
I could never capture the sky
My eyes fake bright blue
So uneven

Another portion of metal
Light up the cigarette
Put on the record
It swims like myths

Leaves crackle like broken glass
When I feel a soul in me
Do I know who is inside
Sometimes it's conflicting

Dishes in the sink
I walk on waterfalls
Upside down in a lake
Silent quiet, quite a place

I remember the sock in my cupboard
My journey into the walls
Footsteps ring in motion
Stating shocks and left commotion

They don't need to speak
This is not for human eyes
There are ghouls and memories
My only thought was to get out alive

Living in the outer ear
My life is spinning clear
Evergreen doesn't grow
Acid feels like flowered snow

The cotton density
Under those bruised lips
Dripping eyelids
What we wanted to be.

ANCIENT BATTLEGROUND

After I delicately decay
I do not mirror great ruins
I was deflowered
Not in bloom
Their walls crumbled
Mine cracked in stages
Too many to replace
My walls are not silent
Bleeding pre-empty
Some withered bones
Are strong enough
To let little cracks grow
And my bones are ravenous
My cracks eat me whole
No other ruin
Has pushed itself to fall
No other ruin
Will break and break
And never fill the cracks on the wall
The cracks
When in reality
There are no cracks at all.

THE HEEL

Do you really intend
On crawling back into that heel
That so willingly divorced you
Birth is troubled, the sounds
Little fingers, tropic eyes
It's a long way down, this time
Like the deep iris of the sea
Watered hope and restless waves
I wonder if the questions talk to the Fates
Some are dead before they talk
Some breathe the answers before they die
A resurrection
When Hades takes the sky
To a flame like your heel has claimed
Burned on your Olympian sun
And nothing else remains

HADES

Approached
A gutter to a million nowhere
A swamp for every soul barer
A king to bare the throne
A prison for the homeless
A life for the lifeless
Does he ever sleep
Is there no rest for his reaper
The after soul sleeper
Of Persephone's dearest keeper
The dreamless waking hour
Hades, the prince
Death's teller
Pouring millions deeper.

ANXIETY

Wasted plain
Sedated, insane
My head amiss
And the hole is not death, if only
The hole sets me down, only to live

There is the cradle
You think you give
It is not holy
It deprives the living
I feel guilty

It is a violent phase
It is a foreign state
It is a home
It is not safe
You crave flesh for a feeding

How comforting is the womb?
I think it breathes
But I don't find the murmur
Maybe because this harmless act
Has turned into murder

Winter snow
Holding on just to be let go
Hoping for a way to stay
Knowing you don't have what it takes
Beheaded, the trauma.

DESCENDANT

Hung
A bunch of faint scars painted
I can't dismiss
Shallow speech on written wrists
I cave into the red eye painted ruins
Beside myself
Your birth to me
I'm still not forgiven
My blood scent
The devils' destined greed
Some homes are savage
Brutal heiress to each of our own
Loveless bodies in rich deformities
Penance to shove it on
Our cross and now we bare it all
The gallows stare and licks their lips
They will bite like ravagers
Hung, they've been staring.

BLUE PRESENTS

You're song is better
I can eat your burnt blood
Save you the pain
Save you the rust
So down, down you go
To better breathe
Mouth corrupt
To live a pretty day
With some bitter rust
Leave your legs to hang
To pull you up
In your tattered heart
The seams are brave
And much too hard
You're craved destruction
Annihilated skin and blue blood
Crawled up ink, a poison shrub
The cavity in a drug
A vein, cracked
A brain, smudged
Your blue antiseptic
Curls up.

MARSH

You leave your stigma
I'll leave mine
We're half wrecked
Soured, denied
Cradled in mother's rye
Debilitated
Tired bones, manic itch
Undelivered
Too raw to arrive
Not parted to leak
The ocean wide
I sleep on the marshes
Sleep the whirlwinds away
Shallow swellings descend
Unkempt, yet alive.

THE PALE FISHERMAN

I've fought against setting moons
I've sought out scarred earthquakes
Even in my most abandoning
The ground was heaviest on my lightest days
I don't feel what I'm after
I don't see who is whom
If it's a failure you are after
You're a riddle, not a clue
Share your helpings
I don't want to shove a finger
And start a war
It seems every out I have
Is put on dial-tone
My body casts out for shore
In sickness I write
In health I stay mute
Is this a sober judgment on my own
The white flag
I guess I don't know
To which the wind goes
The path that unwinds what any of us know
A proper conundrum of quaking hope
Less shell, more rope.

MIDNIGHT INQUIRY

I feel a desperate shape
A corner stone, regretted
If I wrote fondly once the traces of smoke dangle
Portable to no one, least of all me
My born again eyes seem senile by their own right
Wild and riding a storm through my anger
Why do I bother with unfit clouds?
So mild, a stolen world
For the wordless realm of uncertainty
I plague the being of one too many
I spill up and drizzle
I replace the parts that I don't have
And sort through them like aching halves
I've filled myself with a lack of humanity
Drowned myself with the air of insanity
I hemorrhage over my mind
Forever forwarded but ever finished
Neither gawking, but tired
Erased in motion at the core
Lips move and exhaustion radiates
My body blood coils
Shaking off, nod by nod
What pre-exhaustion is living?

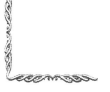

EXHALE

My bruised physician
Tablets on my drawer
The prescriptions you fill
My able lips avoid
Like a poison pressure point
And the sticks I've made
Of bones and pain
Flick their wrists
Cringing towards me
Kissed dumb/blind
To kiss like the injured
So patient and void
Licks blood bright
Brave outside arteries
In waif little cocoons
Borrowed empathy
A grave sign of illness
Famine to my feet
Ingesting a wall of filth
With red taping
On either side of hell
On either side, take me
Make a fossil of my bones
In dark cremated dirt
Of dirt I have risen
Of blood I have died
Of what reason?

HILLS

Scary, open wide
These pills will bleed me dry
On this table I feed my doubts
On this novel of sheets
I leak the drought
In the air that rain swoons
There is ash in my eye
My lungs speak black tar
Like my heart stench the blackest night
Oh, evil has become of me
Loneliness, my host
Of breaking patterns I've become
A sicker sense from time
Of little heart, dear heart of mine
When is this too much to bare
Twenty One years my almost corpse
These days such darker at daylight
What winter this sunshine gives
In this cold grave I fall
In this place I call mine
Twenty One years, there she lays
And it's gathering like a hurricane.

COLOURS

The color scarce
Etches away like dry paint
I'm the impending
Shedding
Picked away

Raging like fireflies
I light all of myself on fire
No. I never burned so brightly
So much softer than the lightning
Ashes burn down my hazards

My mended sores hollow
Blame it all on my half burnt
Half of myself
Tracing the tip of my teeth
I don't feel anything.

Colors, colors
I breathe in colors
Icy as my many memories
A blended fracture
Oh, memories

I call among some
Worst, they drip
Stolen moments
The color of an epidemic
Ours, left behind.

THAT JOURNAL

The falls
Marks, fadelessly haunting
Present rage
Hard to replay
These fears capture everything
I walk to me. Me,
Pages can't be tainted alone
Spoken sheets
What do I do now
Every breath
Spoken on the blank page
Suffocation bruised
The ink a devil's pact.

BALLROOM PARODY

I've got black lungs
Black woes
Black bones, lung bones
Coughing dry
Umbilical wires dried
Dancing

I've got five fingers
Two hurt
Fingers running, jumping
White knuckling
Scattering out
Prancing

I've got a tongue
White hot
Tearing out noise
Barking out surprise
Speaking out
Listless

I've got two arms
Tiny, like worms
Sprouting long lines
Stalking like a harbor tree
Building at the root
Supporting

I've got two eyes
Dawnless, restless things
Traveling inside my skull
Filling its senses dull
Creeping loudly
Foreshadowing.

ANOTHER PIECE

In your own liver
I bury my head
In wicked temperature
Bowel bread

In your linear stomach
Mouthing my meds
Organs fumble
Dark breath

Humming their teeth
Wrinkling inward
Debauched peach
To magnify our failures

Sincere apologies
The rain that engulfs me
Anywhere I bleed
Soft and warm heartbeats

Pricking their finger
Just above my eye
Drowning in crimson
Body parts

Screeching honey seeds
That fill up like bold water
Catching air and breath
And cutting them free

Binge the life
From my worn meat
The epitome
Of birthday cake.

OF MORTEM

Sunlight
A bruise of softer shade
Radiate in radiance
Soft on elbows
Gruesome happenings
Punctured around air holes
A delight
No scar tissue
Shimmering
A pulse of heat
Like water, honey liquid
As if any sense of entitlement
Need no request
To lay inside uninvited
Daylight stares back
And blinds your eyes
Let it take you alive.

BLAND

Caught up in my throat
Hang a rope around my heart
To the fields I roam
Cringing at the sun

My broken age has begun
Sow a bow on to my scabs
Twin arteries that sang
Of blood anatomy I am

On the roof of my mouth
Tender bellies are fed
A scrape of flesh
Some withered empty

Morning silk and gray
Fall has pushed you away
The pain has taken space
We've grown towards distance

I flattered you with words
In my best of faces
I fell afront, aching
With pictured memories

I walk down a tall road
My flesh eaten and flayed
In my heart I beat a stranger heart
This heart beats too hard.

RATHER ACTIONS

Chasing mornings
I faded away
It covered everything
My whole bed still made
Empty, I wake up alone
So don't offer me
A person to breathe on
So I feel a little less mutilated
By the ghost of you
A sour melted ruin
Coated medicine
A disabled cancer
To eat me away
Start from the insides
I'm not so insensitive
My blood is red mortem
I can feel the starvation
The feeling is absolute
No I am not dead yet
How you figured
I wouldn't feel a thing
Melancholy machine.

BLANK ACTIVITY

I let the smoke drown the clean air
Surrounding blank nothings
I've trained myself not to think and just feel
The air cruel against my skins speaks otherwise
I've been numbed to stifling static
Murmuring against my thin flesh
Speaking as it licks against my brain
Growling a silent mantra
It's blood curling to be awake at this hour
This hour is hungry for a feast
The pain is great, it's otherworldly
It hasn't taken over, it has won
My back squirms as if being roasted
I sit up and parts of my bones slide off
They lie where I have lied
Die where I have died
I pull myself upwards, forward and on
Walk like my body parts are full and rich
As if no blood has gone sour
I spoke of the darkness to deaf ears
My eyes are a dry veil
Hushed tones lay on my arms
When these fangs of disease graze down
My simple skin awakes, I am alive.

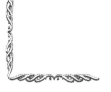

DEVESTATE ME

Virgin eyes
Like a diamond they reflect
Like acid they dissect
Try to drink the holy womb
Raptured baby tooth

Take the pain
Prop the gun
Drop the chain
Use The blood
Drown away from me

Steel touch
Sutured tissue
The veil is off
Can you feel me exclude
I have never been your autobiography

Do you see through me
Or only the drought inside
Smoked bones
I will not have you
No, not I

My head hangs off a tree
Foggy eyes that hold no part of me
For thoughts I once winced
Dust my tie, elegantly envious
The birds have watched us die.

INNOCENT PRESCRIPTIONS

Wound up, out of control
For years I loaded the gun
Took a bullet in the heart
Bled out punctured valentines
Let off my restraints
There's nothing left to die
My heart is blind
Wash the terror from my chest
Erase myself from love
Someone wanted a dime
For every summer dumb
Raised my eyes to the ceiling
Watered rain covered the sun
Want too hard to erase the pain
There's nothing like borrowed suicide
But the pain is a saint
In my clotted eye
Severed women on bicycles
Waving from a disorder tree
Clawed itch, is she still motionless?
Is she a chilled red wine
Picture bodies flying in the night
Crows align in a circle
Won't the sun stop crying?
Stole the marvelous injection
Will it dull my suffering?
Sometimes I just give out and die
While I'm so very much alive
Wandering in the afterlife
While walking under a street light
The poisonous gore reaps my fate
A pale murder, sweet lie.

WITHERING WINDS

God, it tastes good
The swirling filth
Dancing against my tongue
Burning out my lungs
It's like an art of purging
Whiting out the pink buds
Shriveling in the dark
Flowing the dead smoke
Riveting air of dusk
Twirls behind my eyelid
The blister aches like my heart
In the dead swarming night
Crown the arrow of gold
Crippled dove of starvation
A familiar weight
Flesh eating wake
Crevice internal grave
I perish on a star
Much blacker a sun today
Overwhelming venom I cry
And I know an ache like a sigh
What rotten skies fly by.

THE CURRENT

Black pearls, you are so obvious
I taste your perfume like liquid armor
I've never sailed so high
Your tongue licks at my eyes
The clouds of your mouth spread
I am taken towards your frowning eyelashes
What puncture do you hold in your weather clock
I am a shell of mortal value
Hardly enough to devour in cold blood
Predisposed spectacle, my ruby confidant
Have I taken care of no outer hollowed grounds
The pool of your scabs, blister swoon
Poisoned wretch lingering
The taste of crimson teeth, ashen creature
The riveting crowns of boils
You hang beneath my jaw, spoiled.

ATE EIGHT

So they swallowed
Cover up my debris
Why help me when I'm gone
You taste the tinged madness on my tongue
Anyone could just fill in their species
Pretend, regret
As if I exist no less
A full reminder, I stare back.
These days I comfort more than weep
Many countless solemn gazes
I breach them, I reach them
I fade but I still am.
For when I ache you won't defend
I am your lone army
Ever since those bars were framed
So solemn, I was so brave
When you take something
From innocence to break
It stays with you
Reliving my pronounced abortion
Again.

NERVES

Pregnant with ill virus, wilted markings
Stemmed twin umbilical heartbeats
Soft cracked skulls bruised in iron
My sour tasting tongue, I bathe scars there
Licking away at the skin with a weak stare
Light painkiller, you kill me more than death
Tendons are aching adored plastic morphine
With these blood filled gashes I lay down an orphan
Gravel you are a tasteful disguise to die on
Not bound for the living but for the lost
We choke on poisoned waters the taste is astounding
You count all my bones and keep me starving
How brittle you are, your gums chew, mouthing
Inhaling what devil swoons down to earthlings
Carried off into bundled ceilings
A cradle is the farthest away from self-loathing
A beast of medicated teething.

SKELETONS

So serene, too much to bury
Let me take my own heavy heart
A fond place to revisit
To appreciate the violation
The attempts are fragile
You are solid as a rock
I possibly promise to break you
The secret pain I can corrupt
Bloody bones hang from the crib
Extended, carry the breath of wind
I pretend this is not a massacre
I have every ruin of you
Be bled in a cup, the fullest fruit
The bright reflects razors in your eyes
You crawl to the dark and faces arise
Ringing in your ears
The voices you have locked inside
Crawling into fetal position
Shrinking so far out of sight
The skeletons are never ending
The crooked pulp to the skull
My calming invasions.

MEDITATION

Shaped plains
Are where I hid
Summer was cold whisps
Against my ribs
I'm much too small
Winter mold sunken
Beneath my skin
Out in the hole
My frozen friend
The war is within
And we all risk it
Some never again
With a hazardous landing
We grip our lazy blankets
Comforts we never had
Reaching for some warmth
That warms no man
Haunted by the doors
That unlock by chance
Rest in a cradle
Much too big
For my small hands
The outreach
Always out, a trap.

RUFFLES

Written language is the key
My voice only falters
Laces with the whisper
Of the mute

Spoken of borrowed words
Mine feel so tired
Overused
So very full

Mouthing the dreaded
From lips to lips
Luminence
To bleed and swarm

Silver bullets
Serpent of love
Bite the tongue
Burrow in my silence

Sharp wings
Tampered with my skin
Bleeding down on earth
Thunder velvet words

Walls
Feign the vocal chords
Strain with body loss
And dried tissue.

HESITATING

The weight of speaking
Delivering
There are months
They show no growth
So we, steadily
Lose our balancing
And we stop ourselves

Living safely in our ovens
Pre-heated as a casualty
Feeling felt too social
Has there been no actual answer
I carry them
There is no choice
Death can't keep me from tipping

Selfish modern age
Can't take any sort of pain
Forever judged and devoured
Living for that swollen vein
The words slow and sound
They save nothing
Just another stain to save for the winter

SIGH

I let the rope blood sing
Like a virus
I leak of poisoned skin
And dead violence
And the noose swings brave
In clotted iris

A waste of salted wine
Serial eyes
A breached infant spine
The twin ripeness
Can almost feel them breathe
In the night

Sown in the hollowed grave
Wings spun
Weathered insane
So I held the blade
Swindled brain
And withered lies

The winter face
The crown of illness
Cleans the pain off my wrists
Swallowed inside
Carried
The pulsed swamp of bliss

Soundly injured
Caught in my face
I lie
Widowed in age
Inside
Haunted iodine.

OUR RELAPSE

At what point are we judged?
How many mouthfuls are too full?
I would have died, I would have pruned

My bathed environment is scar tissue
I wrap it up and smile over rescue
It's been so long, raw skin lights up

The pain is roasting a feast of life
The pain is fizzling a pointless climb
The scars I'm making are twice abused

When I call out you sail too soon
My blood is drowning, a dull platoon
My body appalls me with skin too smooth

If treatment is crawling my knees are bruised
For once I am calling to no one's tune
The house of my longing weaves a noose

I clung in hope, two white strings
The rain keeps falling
And where are you?

NO SUCH GOODBYE

Soft rose bed
Sometimes she polishes
The air I felt was gray
And every summer
I wished her summer away
Flowers, naked petals
I needed her so much
More than she could take
My melting memory
Dead as well as she
Cracks and breaks
Now she's more like me
She ran away
Ran away from me
I don't see her from where I stand
I bleed for her to come back
She has the biggest part of me
And now I'm lost eternally
I wished her summers away
So she's stay frozen
So she'd stay
She dies anyway
Her rose bed covers the sheets

MASS

Its loss of shape
Animated
Like the gloves
Powdered like a baby
Wreaks a lie
As if innocence was picked
Hand palms coolly
Straight, wise holy bargain
Time replays no end
Still wasted in gloved hands
Bottoms-up
Face to mind
Talk of conspiracy
Have they half walked
Tied shoes or off
Ten times bigger in sight
Hollow price
How much apart
Me or mine.

SENTIMENT

I fade on rumbled sheets
They've been miles and miles
In my skin, my sickness
They have sucked the punctured ebb
Left unscarred in red bellied fullness
Thickened and spread out
And lays down eggs in the lands I fear
They cave of cobweb heathen blood
These rumbled sheets sob
And bury these broken embryos
These walls must fall
Until there's nothing left at all
Where was the dark
When I needed despair
Where was the blood
When I felt nothing there
I wish I was above
Suffocating myself with unwellness
Locked inside
The white ruin, so much sharper
Devoured, mouth bitter
The act of my action
So strong nor can I avoid
Whispers mouthed in the dark.

THE ROOM KEEPER

What was falling
Is it the sight of your every eye
Was it truth
Growing in your iris veil

When you look back
They're superior
Buds of escapism
Cradle sanctum

You realize what you do
Can I ever feel enough to feel you?
You burst brazen, fool
Oh dear, we need dusting in this room.

SERPENTINE

Is the world any less compelling
When the den is thick
In frustration, anger, and bitterness
Is the ship unsinkable
If we never tire to let it be?
Giant watchtower
Lay awake in the land of my troubles
Tall and pondering
How little and small I really am
In a world I have no hand
A maze of desperate land
I am grown to learn
My childhood is a leaking aftermath
It floods around
Engulfs what I am
And still I am too little
To save them from their own hand
Then the escape lulls
Not into wellness—only into fear.

HARMING

I've seen your petals dry
Meek and lonely things
With wanting, I retaliated

The lit match spoiled
Sweet bitter mouthfuls
An etched mourning

The scales collapse down the wall
Onto my flattered floor
The grand applause

It's been days
I have run myself raw
The meat sticks to the skin like gasoline

With a dream of warm meat
I dreamt quite a scene
I was unraveling

A big chunk/small chunk
All tucked away with me
The taste is of youth

As I lay down on the death bed
I breathe in the drugged sponge
And I see my scars.

THE BLUE LAKE

Blinded wounds
Solid mind fallen
Consumed, the breaking
How do we eat
They fall from outer muscles
Torn ligaments
For days
So we detail our eyes
Constant leaks
For I have no remorse
Walk, my fingers shook
A shovel, newly forgiven
Aligned
So to speak
They sold all but me
So ashamed
A quiet lake
To hold my misery
Walk as if owned
Flushed
Dark wired
Tired, so tired
No right
Blooming.

BLACK FOG

The darkest vowel, none spoken
Naked for all of them to use
Tears on bloodied tissue
It's not a breath but a coffin laid in you
You have burnt my sound
My eyes drip, splattering
Everything will cave in—chaffed
The empty pit I have rotted in
Smoke drips down my spine
My burnt ribs mirror the back of my eyelids
In your arsenal heart I beat
Stale closure falls beneath your feet
I can't be your messenger
Kissed alive in your eyes, a pulse carved
Lingering wounds of my first infliction
Your raindrops on my flesh
I sow the sin, body skin of beauty
Coma too far to amend
Wreaking stomach juice
The carnage parasite.

TARANTULAS

My ghost skin ripples
With aftereffect
Grinning in attention
Another two faced deflection
Integrated
Personal self-instigations
I have let myself be led
By heart I feel too closed in
By head I throw up repression
And mortality scrapes
It claws down my hand
I close my eyes
And they climb.

SWELLING GAUZE

My body slurs
Cinnamon injuries
What a pretty mess I've made
Scarlet lips, fingerprints on the wall
Write my pain in savage whispers
My abyss sinking you
In my sober eyes
As if you could save yourself
You've drowned all over me
Grown into sloppy demons
I haven't felt a beat, nor a pulse
Where my skin is your own to dissect
I forgot how to choke
Until you made me breathe
I broke like jewels
In front of inhuman eyes
The swollen star pouring misery
Flooding my heart
I've been dead here all too long
Drunk on wasted utopia
Each piece, sweet sores
I lie awake and I burn.

SOUR WAKE

Sour cake, my aching dress
I swam in silence
Drowned in the abyss
Sharp inhaled gasps
Picture yourself
Faint in a grave
And soft aching cells
I'm fed, I'm fed
Hair tangles around your neck
Sweet pain, fully undressed
My arms gather
Sharp grass slicing my flesh
Bouncing red light
Paint like distress
A mouthing silent membrane
Calling out for your regret
But I have loads to carry
And I'm crushing to bits
Only hope leaks a mess
Salvation runs down the drain
Like my split vein
Body taken, rebel insane
Death, I've taken your last name.

SELF-POLLUTION

Quilted
Soft under the sedative
My urine floral
Damnation bride
My dead adore

Shells
Pale core
A pulsed bitter marrow
Soft limbs, almost anorexic
As empty shells

Home is an asylum
A vitamin escape
Sells the person in me
Unknown face
A puncture scab

Bandage carver
A present
Self-nemesis
Sick melodies
Something unseen.

LITTLE ME

I feel it breathe
And it's not enough
For this hole in me
I've paid too much
To walk alone
The deal is done
I ached out in swirls
And baby blood
My eyes, bleak raisins
Cold as ice
Every heart in seams
I never had mine
Burning faith
It's like murder
And to what disguise
Do I
Fading much deeper
Crystal sulfur
It rains down
On my rabid palm
I created a temper
And I wished you
You would pray
To a devil I own
I can't walk away
To the ether I belong
Tarnished wings
I have in vain
Blood clot heroin
Belittle me.

INFIRMITY

I can't force a better self
Complaint
My own indents have more nakedness
Than my virus
I pounce
Like burrowed trash
These instigators own my pistol
I am so afraid they will
Claw my soft red bladder
So distinct in my own delusion
It is the only purging absolution
I am disappointed
My own waste is so plain
No digesting will color the meat
I am desperate to taint
For the love of penance
Please take me over
Serve my purpose a dyed servant
And I will myself to eat
A more digestive soup.

BONES

Don't reply
I'm not savage like you
They stick out like blades
My lone escape

No one can see
Skin so diseased
Please look between
My brain is stuffed

Splendid towards a body stencil
Porcelain to the bone
Tinker bell, small and sterile
Take a bath in it

My body retains bothered meat
Walking a tight-rope
To see my insides grow
Only to be so unimproved

Withering in plain sight
A body so unpleased as mine
Taking every map to find you
Sinking deeper towards no wellness

BLEAKEST CROWN

The edge, price payer
A dream of splendid lights
Of bringers like you
How cheap raw thoughts I own
Have never seemed so reverent
Have never seemed so bold
As the tip of the icy tongue of murder
Of the breath I stink of
Oh, shower of dead thoughts
Blundering in the wind
Of what feast have I become
An ill-tempered jailor
Hearts of cut down marrow
In beneath these solar roots
Non-bathed cuticles
Rough to the touch
The outpour disgust
Oh, queen Demeter
What have I done?
To thirst on your own crown
As I bleed all over the soil
Making murder your descent
Soaking all earth in red boils
Priceless keeper
Hovered and cowering.

SELFLESS AIM

Pressure points unearth, her
Cliché tangled in birth
Cannibal scent, the bred coat
Carnivore soaked, the blood rope
Tear the blood off my marrow
Let the sleeves of my bones
Kiss the tissue of my scars
Of bloody binges incarnate
Infants of my heart
Wet lingering mouth sores
A deepened rattled marsh
Of blowing whistles in the dark
A candle bristles like a heart
Serpent slithers
Around and apart
The edge is nearer
I can feel the needles gape
As I sit and yet I wander
Of battled blood
Would I have to wake
In a crushed mortal incense
And prey on my own skeleton
To quench the thirsted ache
Burning alone like alcohol
Carrying on with a mouth
Half gashed, engraved
Little helpings of past wrath
And devastation in my veins.

PLIANT CAGES

Caged up
Lock those broken hearts
We don't need more raindrops
Soft end lips are trembled
Such a bleak affection
Felt the moon was washed
I guess I took too many
Farther than I was, you were
Can you hear her
Lovely shade, heartless blade
Such a shame for my companion
So we cut the swallowed mist
It sprinkles on our bodies
Felt nothing from my own, devoured
The innocent, too many
Bitten, scotch still burning
Caught beneath his infection
Blood is bored
My taste has faults
Soured plenty.

CASSANDRA

Careful now—I cry
Stumbled dumb like I tasted a fool
A radiant hue
Maternal haze
I related to you
Junk devoured, swallowed
Years ago
I feel it crawl
Ages of pain—devil flu
I can feel my own pain
Inside of you
Reach and tie our bow
Hang around—neck tied
Black and blue
Reach and hang
Eternal platoons
Karma stinks
Through your roots
Aches all rotten
Felt my drain
Succumb passage
After horizon perfume
Sour—even with angel fluid
My bone rubbing tissue
Sharper deaths glare
As I starve over you
Felt my pain
Said I felt my pain inside of you.

PAGES

Hail fell like the Gods today
Like your eyes are watching
Dead and glistening
Walking by with Death
Watch him speculate
Eyes not pale
So many lives
Why not mine?

You leave me pages of tears
With nothing but blank air
I can't catch you
Even if I tried
Cold rooms
All the silence
Pages of a room
No pieces
You've locked my doors

No reality
No proof
The person, if you
Every night colored blue
Calm, nothing new
Pastures I've lied on
And yet
Pages on my drawer
No trace of human shoes

Sought you a long way down
Craving the desperate invitations
Pages on my bed
Pages of agonized regret
Something only I could represent
I reap too soon.

THE LOVELORN

I'm ill and half hearted
A creature with sickened blood
Took every pill I had to find you
I said I wouldn't be too long
I cradled you in fine madness
The chalk of winds I came to love
I bore the innocence of halos
You tear it down for me
I reached above and down below
I found too little of my soul
White hail rain is still descending
Knocking wilted pain on my window
I wish they wouldn't scream of angels
I know they don't exist anymore
You paint a picture to surround me
As if I had no other way
And now I see my weak bandage
I walk a heart of crippled veins
I've fallen so much farther than you
I'm too heavy to pick up my disgrace
I face the faces that surround me
The acid weight of yesterday
So sweet and soft the snow is sprouting
Like a flower only cold and cruel
Your scent is everywhere around me
I'm starting to believe that you aren't true
Please stop your voice from dancing
I've not of sound mind I cannot go
So precious you are in your features
Bones so sharp I could scrape my own
Your entire mind is full of demons
And I can relate with your sorrow
Breathing through your gas chamber
A poisoned hello will do
If I bring up my own disaster
Your lips mark my wounds in blood

Just a taste I can believe
And it's so sad that our destroyer
Is the mind I've come to believe
So I sit back in my confinement
And try to will away my misery
To take these pills and stop the dreams

SOWN HOME

Waif and obvious
Glittered black wink
You dare to throw
I like your little arms
Feasted bones
What complex nectar
Your ill garden grows
You growl, my confidant
The rumble reeks
A poisoned hello
Scattered on my pillow
I deflect like broken mirrors
To me you are like ash
A touch is too bold
Twin alien stares
My neck wound
Splits your head
And what a heart
A shriveled bow
Too tired so suffocate
Myself on my own
Your blood tempered
A divine specimen
No name fits you
Your words drip
They grow in my bones
My heart, once mine
Has sown itself a home.

THE CLOCK'S LITTLE HAND

I wished someone would teach me love
To avoid the way my already narrow eyed heart
Clots and aches in drugged blood
I'd raise my eye in positions
As if had that role
But now I go down that sweet skin, lying
Stenches, and I know my own oats
If I'd be barren to the outcome
It'd feel bittersweet
My watered milk is too long soaked
I despair in my own moist cave
And there is no kingdom
That will lay down to heal
The desperate arms have hallowed in me
I have no forth coming kismet soul to bestow
And my purest energy weeps on my own pillow
What I rejoice and the pain
Isn't the undoing I hold
Pull me apart
The stench of cigarette ashes
Remember the last golden glance
Ruining my high again
Grinding me down again
Away to all our debris
My own outer subconscious
Should have made that distance
Crossed those ocean eyes
Blazed among that frozen sky
Dared to dream while you were alive
Songs paint many ghosts
The letter of nevers almosts
A rush I won't feel
When the light erodes
A birth stilled, farther alone.

DOUSED

My posh alliance
Cluttered in my staged liaison stove
Prisoner
So claustrophobic
Highs so precocious
I am a lead pencil
I turn into fetus juice
Sprouting like amnesia
Pleasantry is dead
I am held skeptic
They speak in tongues
But you have your own source of infliction
I can only remember the guilt of being
The one I wish was whole
You are liable, my medical Freud
It is you who know
Fraud.

ALEXANDER

We're drawn to each other
Half looking
And never finding
We're damned to each other
Neither pure
Both purged and ever dying
We're lost with each other
One with no host
The other with no soul
We're wounded to each other
Lighted ablaze
In the pool of lightning
We're bound to each other
Stapled veins
Strangled hearts
We've annihilated one other
A pretty puncture, my darling sang
I bet a bullet would help.

POLLINATION

Coralline feet
I follow him
I stalk towards
I stalk beneath
Watch in bewilderment
I fall in love, tiny wrists
To envelope, bambi lips
Posh liver specs
Cradled in dangling arms
Your icicle brown membrane
I do body blood shame
Air as thick as swallowed pebbles
Twin eyelid pennies
To tempt brands of ill weepers
And drag a somber swirling mess to bay
Taking baby legs and pushing forward
With black large bones

SO HE CLAWS

Wild like the sea
Crumbled nothings
The next timed, the sufferer
My heart still
Scrubbed so hard
Little pieces
Sprinkled in the deep
Fallen stains
Sinking burials
Crooked simile
Washed away in pieces
So what if the pure weren't as filthy as me
Swallowed
Don't grieve, don't grieve
He's lonely, he's spoken.

CRAVEN

You should be drowned
Delightfully drowned
Your arrogance, and the way you dry
Swirl like bitter wine
The ways you start off high
And how you crash louder than God
Those roses and ribbons pale in comparison
And those scars aren't fooling anyone
Drowning in your river bed
We kept pulling you out
And so I guess being you
It takes its toll
Cause it sure rapes you now
Dull and boring in the graveyard
And nothing to say
You throw yourself over them
And try to bury yourself beneath
And where did all that strength come from
You barely will a breath
And I think I saw your anger
I think that's what your pain is
Shut off all their blame
Shut off all their lies
I see your eyes ravenous
I guess you had it right
I can only rid you dry
Thrown, wrap you obscenely
Shoulders slumped
Carry you to an alcove burial
Where the dirt is bloodlust
A fine burnt smell
Be it the roof of my body
To cave in as well.

SOLD

My cracked smile
My swollen tooth
Spent it all
Spent it all on you
I bathed in fire
I bathed in truth
See what damage
You can do

I've bitten carnage
I've bitten you
Sent you death
And I sold you

You've tasted the gutter
You've tasted glue
You've tasted rotten water
That I gave you
I gave you rapture
I gave you a thousand moons
You ate them all
And I threw them out for you

I've bitten carnage
I've bitten you
Sent you malice
And I sold you

Tear me up something new
I've tasted all your filth
You precious cannibal
You've taken all I gave to you
And now the sun, fully bruised
She's taken off her lights
To breed blind for you
Such a pretty sight for you

I've bitten carnage
I've bitten you
Sent you the power
So you sold me too.

BITTER LEMONADE

Your heart ate
Can't amputate
Sinking deeper than I ever thought I could
You are an injured blot of sun

Can't quite abort the blood
Suffering is your brand of love

The bond will break
I stumble and I ache
You are a force of violence
With arrogance, charm, and grace

Blossomed black coals and lies
Wilting flames depict your eyes

I blame you
A challenge I can abuse
Intoxicating with just one bruise
Three words can stab at broken wounds

You just drag it out
Prolonged the damage we ache to soothe

You could never be comforting
As I could never tell you the truth
A torturous wave
I've fallen, I'm yours to use

I bit my lip and it bled blue
The taste is stale, it tastes like you.

SOCIOPATHIC INTUITION

I dig my roots underneath your heart
Selfless as it is
It's quite a sadistic art

I don't trust what I see
It's an illusion
Waiting to capture me

This is a trap
A vision above instinct
Strip me of my skin

Pain
That's what you call life
I won't disagree

I know there's a reason
A flaw you wish to expose
Everything is a conspiracy

A lie
Collateral consequence
A challenge, how devoted you are

You are very accurate
You look me in the eye
For a moment I believe, the puncture and the lie

There is nothing that comes for free
Fear makes you vulnerable
Pieces make up what you see

Do you feel warm inside? Happy?
Shackles at your feet
Lines and scrapes, I wear corruption on my sleeve.

SMITTEN

Cigarette ash tastes twice as sweet
Than berries or flower nectar
The drunken pollen of ill weather
A lung of acid is spring
A mouthful of iron is summer
A vein of heroin is fall
A bullet is winter and I take it all
A shape of hell is my interval
Down again in the same swirl
A wretched name I have to call

Don't bleed in me, don't bleed in me
I have no poison to give
It's all in my lead burnt veins
And I don't forgive you at all

I take a careful indent
And I burn it like a dream
Take the smell of your flesh
The barren skin I have walked in
I am taken to small sins
A devil's drink on my bland lips
And I, I can't recall
What heaven is red
What evil is sweet
And what murder I am of them all

Don't bleed in me, don't bleed in me
I have no poison to give
It's all in my dead gnawed lips
And I don't forgive you at all

I impersonate because I am ill
I am a person to hate
I am a person to love
I am anything but well
I am gone, I am gone
You reek of swan petals
The epitome of wellness
I am not well, not well at all
Here's a piece of my shallow skin
The skin is burnt raw

Don't bleed in me, don't bleed in me
I have no poison to give
It's in my wicked skin
And I don't forgive you at all.

ABSENT

Some years slide off my lungs
And you come home to borrow
The only waste of battle blood
So I'm crawling back through mud
I drift further down through you
I pour out the like anger you swam of
Did you wait through the rain?
Did you scar yourself again?
Look through your glass eyes
And drown with me, doused in me
You breathe colder than winter
And everything turns black to white
Tearing all of me, all I am
Your kiss stings of broken marrow
Drips of bones sharp as glass
And your barrel of creations
The sickness reeks of burnt hands
Invasive scalpels paint around your back
Screaming sedative, deeper down
Once they've patched up the black
Changeling, you have been bruised
And I in turn, bruise through you

VOLATILE

I birthed a fire and watched it burn
Immersed in blood and ill shattered trauma
Volatile sunken mess
Pour jugular juice under your dress
You walk on my drawn strings
Devouring every pound of my black bile
Torn out from ligaments
Sticking to the bone until it's been purged
Until I feel it in every inch
The cycle of the mad
Drowsy ink splattered bread
Cancer tree, swaying like a new halo
To divide my flesh from my bone
Grief plush and decorated
Bland to my simple dead roots
Festering soil, damp and ruined
Like my scarred marrow
Quilt of barren anger fill my wounds
Until I turn it inward, a brittle tomb
Caskets swim in my disorder lullaby
Breathing ripe every night
So burn little fleshlings, burn until you're white
Burn until the skies fall down tonight
Cradle me in my death bed
Where I lie ashen and pruned
Flayed with flower gasoline
I'm tangled in a crib with slaughtered wings

RAVAGED MUTE

The pain on my lips is grand
The pain on my lips have grown arms
The pain on my lips makes everything
Feel like nothing at all
The pain on my lips
Starts falling like burning stars
The pain on my lips
Are churning in rewritten scars
The pain on my lips
Is carrying the screams
To the land of unspoken mouths
The pain on my lips
Bury me like body parts
The pain on my lips
Need removal.

BEDSIDE

Lean on
The picture falls hollow
The earth pitch dark
And foot soles in arch

Lean on
The devil wears red
Sniffing around my head
Saving grace for blood

Lean on
The dampest eye wink
Sheltered and malevolent
Creaking at every crack

Lean on
My hand chafed
I'm holding on too long
The ground zeroes in

Lean on
I tried to trick the tracks
The edge of the world
Hollers

Lean on
My individual
The day is half black
My throat wrung empty

Lean on
To suffer in the light
Hold on a bit too tight
Bless you sleeplessness.

WOLF

You sound so raw and desperate
The impending pulled back to the present
Vocal chords bleeding and wretched
What year did you last speak?

You lay down in dark space
The matter has gone
All afloat in the eerie whisper
What year did you last slumber?

You rave in your ravenous winter
Talk of incidents with splendor
Of massacre and murder
What year did you last bleed?

You hunt with a tongue swaggering
Like a man possessed
Digging and clawing in my bed
What year did you last hunger?

You found a nest
A bundle of great youth
Terror in your heart and hands
What year did you last murder?

You lap at the poor wrist
Dangling out with marrow
I sneeze and you proceed
What year did you last capture?

You breed the toughest breed
A brood of little restraint
And you tear about my heart
What year did you last howl?